INTO DAYLIGHT

Into Daylight.
Copyright 2014 Jeffrey Harrison. All rights reserved.

Library of Congress Cataloging-in-Publication Data

Harrison, Jeffrey.
[Poems. Selections]
Into daylight / Jeffrey Harrison. — First paperback edition.
    pages cm— (The Dorset Prize)
ISBN 978-1-936797-43-1 (pbk. original : alk. paper)
I. Title.
PS3558.A67133I53 2014
811'.54—dc23

Cover and text designed by Howard Klein.
Cover photograph by Chris Landry. Used with permission.

First paperback edition: April 2014.

Tupelo Press
P.O. Box 1767
243 Union Street, Eclipse Mill, Loft 305
North Adams, Massachusetts 01247
Telephone: (413) 664–9611 / Fax: (413) 664–9711
editor@tupelopress.org / www.tupelopress.org

Tupelo Press is an award-winning independent literary press that publishes fine fiction, nonfiction, and poetry in books that are a joy to hold as well as read. Tupelo Press is a registered 501(c)3 non-profit organization, and we rely on public support to carry out our mission of publishing extraordinary work that may be outside the realm of large commercial publishers. Financial donations are welcome and are tax deductible.

NATIONAL
ENDOWMENT
FOR THE ARTS
Supported in part by an award from the National Endowment for the Arts

For Jeremy and Ellen

Contents

I

II

III

IV

FOR CLARE

I saw a brown shape in the unmown grass,
half-hidden in a tuft, and crouching down
to get a closer look, I found a young rabbit,
no bigger than my hand, trembling there
in its makeshift nest. And I thought of John Clare:
this was one of his creatures in my own yard,
pressed close to the earth, timid and alone,
almost a visitation from the "bard
of the fallow field and the green meadow,"
who loved the things of nature for what they are.
It didn't run away when I parted the grass
and stroked its soft fur, but quivered in fear,
the arteries in its small translucent ears
glowing red, its dark eyes wide. I thought
of keeping it, at least for a few days,
feeding it bread and lettuce, giving it water
from an eye dropper. Then it did run away
in little bounds to the edge of the woods,
and into the woods. I thought again of Clare,
how, after he escaped from the asylum,
he walked almost a hundred miles home,
lost, delusional, beyond anyone's care,
waking soaked in a ditch beside the road,
so hungry that he fed himself on grass.

Out Back

The ferns, mint, foxglove, and tall grass
growing every whichway behind the kitchen
surpass anything I could say
about them. And the purple vetch
I pulled out yesterday—
perhaps I was wrong to think
it was strangling the others;
it might just as well have been
binding them all together ...
though here I could be making yet
another mistake. Better to let them
all be, to take of them freely
by other means and without
much remark, the way the wind
bends and jostles the ferns,
and the bumblebees and moths
visit the last pink bells at the tops
of the swaying foxglove stalks.

I

SEPARATION ANXIETY

I don't know where my thoughts were that day walking through the woods—
maybe with my brother who had killed himself a few months earlier,
or maybe trying to avoid that, obsessively focused on something else,
or caught on the treadmill of an imagined argument
with a friend who'd told me he was afraid
I was writing about my grief rather than feeling it—
but when I came back to where I was and turned around on the trail

the dog was gone. I called his name: nothing. I kept calling
and retraced my steps to the place where three trails crossed.
It was inexplicable how quickly I began to panic,
how quickly calling turned into screaming, and then weeping,
except that it made perfect sense. And there was also my son,
home sick from school, who didn't like to be left alone,
though that is what I'd done. The longer it took to find the dog,

the more I felt his fear. When, some half an hour later,
the dog seemed to just appear, I fell to my knees
in the muddy path and hugged him, repeating his name,
as if he'd returned from the dead, then ran with him on his leash
the mile or so to where the car was parked and drove home,
where I found my son just as I'd imagined him, sobbing,
unable to speak, as when I'd told him his uncle was dead.

Before the Play

Before the play, my friend and I had dinner
at a small French bistro near the theater.
It had only been three months since my brother
had killed himself, and three months felt like nothing,
but I was doing my best to tell him what I could.
What I didn't expect was when my friend asked me
how he'd done it. Something in me tightened.
I had promised my brother, or his memory,
that I wouldn't reveal that to anyone.
Maybe it was the wine, or that I hadn't seen my friend
since it had happened and needed his sympathy,
but I haltingly stepped up to the edge
of that precipice, and then took one more step.
I was in the middle of telling him
when he held up his hand and stopped me
mid-sentence. At first I thought he was saying
I didn't have to go on if it was too hard,
but then I saw his face brighten with expectancy,
his green eyes looking up and following
whoever it was passing behind my seat . . .
a famous actress, he explained, not seeing
what must have been the look in my own eyes,
caught as he was in a thoughtless moment,
one kind of curiosity giving way to another—
which left me hanging, having to force myself
to finish telling him what he wanted to know.

ENCOUNTER WITH JOHN MALKOVICH

When I spot him in Tower Records, two aisles over,
flipping through bins of discounted CDs
at their going-out-of-business sale, his shaven head
half-covered by the hood of his gray sweatshirt,

my first thought is I want to tell my brother,
but my brother is dead. And yet I watch him furtively,
searching for some Malkovichian quirk,
some tic that might make Andy laugh,

but he isn't giving anything away
besides his slightly awkward stoop over the racks.
Then it comes to me that if I can't tell my brother
about John Malkovich, I can tell John Malkovich

about my brother, and my heart starts pounding.
Normally, I don't believe in pestering celebrities,
but there are exceptions: if Spalding Gray
walked in right now, I would definitely talk to him—

but that's impossible, since he, like my brother,
though under very different circumstances,
killed himself. But John Malkovich is alive
and standing right over there, and my mind

is racing ahead to the two of us leaving
the record store together, then having coffee
at a nearby diner, where I am already
telling him how my brother was obsessed

with the movie of Sam Shepard's *True West*
and especially with him, John Malkovich,
playing Lee, the older of two brothers;
how Andy, who was my older brother,

loved to imitate Malkovich, or rather Lee,
everything from his small off-kilter mannerisms
to his most feral outbursts—but even then
he'd be smiling, unable to hide his delight;

and how, every Christmas, he brought the video
to our parents' house in Ohio, and our parents
would groan when they walked through the room,
and sigh, "Not this again," or call it

"the most unChristmassy movie ever made."
Which is probably true. But for us—him and me,
our other brother and our sister, but especially him—
you'd have to say it was our *It's a Wonderful Life.*

And I have to tell him how Andy used to cue the tape up
and ask, "Can we just watch this one scene before—"
before whatever it was we were about to do,
go out for dinner or visit our demented grandmother,

and we'd watch him, John Malkovich, standing on a chair
shouting pronouncements, or destroying a typewriter
with a golf club, and we'd go off laughing and exhilarated
to our appointed errand, his inflections ringing in our ears . . .

But now it's something about the way he thoughtfully
considers his purchases, shuffling through them,
then putting one back, reconsidering, his hand
hesitating over the bins, that somehow reminds me

of Andy, and makes me certain Malkovich
would be interested in him, a sympathetic character
if there ever was one: funny, gentle,
a lover of dogs and kids (who had neither),

with an odd sense of humor and some mostly unobtrusive
symptoms of obsessive compulsive disorder,
who, like Lee, but to a much lesser degree (or so
we thought), had trouble placing himself in the world—

a part I'm certain Malkovich could play,
all of it coming full circle, Malkovich
playing Andy playing Malkovich playing Lee,
or just Malkovich playing Andy, bringing him

back to life, the way Lee suddenly springs
back up at the end of the movie, alive
after all, menacing as death, the phone cord
still wrapped around his neck . . .

It turns out that John Malkovich and I
do leave the store together: we check out
at the same time, two registers apart,
then head for the door, the moment coming

to a peak for me as I realize my last chance
is about to slip away. But Malkovich, in front of me,
has to wait there while a stream of people coming in
briefly blocks his exit, and I watch, in profile,

his flurry of impatient blinking—or is it a display
of exaggerated patience?—each blink counting off the seconds
he is forced to wait, or the number of customers
going by him, not recognizing him, it seems to me,

though his hood is down by now. And I think,
this is it, this little fit of blinking is the thing
Andy would delight in most, the one detail
he would rewind the tape to see again.

Two Salukis

I wanted to tell you about the dogs we saw
on a sunny day in Berkeley, California,
a few years back while traveling with the kids:
two princely, sleek salukis that promenaded
on leashes past the glinting café tables
off Telegraph, where we happened to be sitting.

It wasn't just the dogs I wanted to tell you about
but also the man with long matted gray hair
sitting nearby—perhaps afflicted
with Asperger's, perhaps homeless—who blurted,
"Those are beautiful dogs!" then shouted almost in anger,
"They're better than people!—better than people!"

And for a startled moment we teetered
between uneasiness and hilarity,
then went with the latter: that repeated phrase
became the refrain of our afternoon,
the kids and I riffing on it to a hip-hop beat
as we wandered around campus and strolled the streets.

And while we were reeling off our badly rhymed couplets,
I could almost hear your antic voice joining in,
as if you were speaking through us
or we were keeping alive that part of you
you couldn't hold onto in the end and we too
lost sight of after you so suddenly

left us: your playfulness, the way
you'd latch on to a phrase and repeat it
like an absurd mantra, or make up songs
with dogs as heroes, and sing them to the dogs—
almost as if you were trying to tell them
they were better than people.

ESSAY ON A RECURRING THEME

For a long time I wrote only about my brother,
or, more accurately, about his death
(okay, his suicide), but to this day
some five years later, I still don't know
if I understand anything more now
about why he killed himself, or even

about my own feelings, or whether I even
should have written those poems about my brother,
or if I should be writing this one, now.
Did writing them help me to "cope with his death,"
allow me to "work through it"? I don't know.
Or was I only putting off the day

I could "move on," or (the opposite) some day
of reckoning I couldn't face? I couldn't even
tell you which. But writing is what I know
how to do, so I wrote about my brother,
worrying that it was too much his death
I was writing about, as I still worry now,

and feeling guilty, as I still do now,
that I'd exposed the awful privacy of that day
by trying to make "art" out of his death.
One friend said he feared I was even
writing the experience of grief for my brother
instead of living it. I thought: What does he know?

There wasn't a choice between them, and there was no
way of disentangling one from the other. Now,
I see that all those poems about my brother
were the opposite of waiting for a day
to look back in tranquility or even
just sadness. I had no distance, and his death

was huge, and I was inside it. His death
was black and swirling, and I didn't know
how to ride those savage currents, or even
what to do or think or feel. And now?
The distance helps. But there will never come a day
when I reach some final word about my brother.

There's not a day that I don't think about his death.
Some days, I don't even know how to be.
Oh, brother, tell me what I should do now.

TEMPORARY BLINDNESS

It lasted a year and a half,
as if grief had closed an inner lid
between my eyes and brain
or slipped a caul over my head.

I spent my days in the black space
inside me, orbiting a dead star.
Now I want to return to earth.
I want to come back from the dead,

to remove the sack from my head
and breathe again,
and let the world in—

here, now, right in front of me—
to be awakened by a lake
glittering through trees.

LEARNING THE TRAILS

Jobless, confused, off-kilter from another move,
the lines I scribbled in my blue notebook
going nowhere, trailing off on pages
mostly blank, I'd get up from my desk
and set out to explore the township's woods.
It was not "the solace of nature" I was after
but a project to occupy me, and it became
an obsession: weeks of getting lost
on those tangled trails unmarked but for
an occasional cairn of horse droppings.
Without map or compass I walked
for miles each day, so that my aching legs
would wake me at night, and when I did sleep
I dreamed of walking trails and getting lost.

Over and over I came to an open meadow
where tall grass rippled along dips and swells
that sloped down to a blue-green pond, and up
to an old bench under a lone white pine.
It should have been enough for me to find
that genial place, but I was not content
to sit for long and made myself go on
and enter the woods on the far side
where a silver stirrup hung from a tree branch
by its leather strap, like an odd sign.
But beyond the meadow I was hopeless.
It played tricks on me, turned everything askew,
as if the meadow were the hub of that whole countryside
and would twist on its axis and get me lost.

Some poets seem to have an epiphany
every time they take a walk, but that's not
what this was like. I walked fast, paused
only to brush the deer ticks off my pant legs,
and usually I was sweating, even after fall
began to slip into winter. I was never
where I thought I was, and my surroundings
never connected into metaphors except
in their lack of connection, the trails
that made no sense or fizzled out.
Even when I noticed something beautiful—
the crinkled asterisks of witch hazel in bloom
or a stand of beech trees flickering
their pale leaves—I couldn't take it in.

But gradually I learned the trails. I bought
a compass, took notes, tied bits of yarn
to saplings, drew little maps on scraps of paper.
One day when I was describing to a friend
how I'd walked clear into the next town
without crossing a road, I heard an old note
of enthusiasm in my voice and realized
I was getting somewhere. We don't like
to admit that possession matters to us,
but it wasn't until I felt those woods becoming mine
that I began to feel anything, or to see
without the map in my head blinding me—
slowing my pace and looking around,
finding a rhythm, longing for song.

KINGFISHER

Megaceryle alcyon

I hear the kingfisher before I see him,
chattering as he makes his rounds
along the lakeshore, then landing on a dead branch
not far from where I'm sitting on the dock.
Only if I'm lucky will I see him dive.

He could be the emblem of this mild place
(halcyon being part of his name) disturbed
by nothing but his rattling call, a dog
barking over the water, human voices
smoothed to intonations, and a rippling

uneasiness that blows through me in gusts
like an unpredictable crosswind
from the world I've left behind for a week,
or the recollection that it was grief
that transformed Halcyon into a kingfisher.

CUSTODY OF THE EYES

Gerard Manley Hopkins

To look at the world
with devotion,
giving all of himself
to what was given,
sometimes gave him
so much pleasure
he thought it must be
a sin, distracting him
from his devotion
to God. Therefore
the eyes had to be
taken into custody
like a pair of criminals,
kept in the flesh-and-
bone cell of the head,
their gaze cast down
in penitence,
the eyes themselves
watched over
to prevent them from
looking at anything
more than was needed
to get through the day.
For weeks or months
at a time, and once
for half a year,
he denied himself
the beauty he knew
more acutely than others,
as if reducing each thing—
flower, stone, bird—
to a single word,

stripping it of the
singularity
he loved to describe
in rushing phrases
that spilled down
his journal's pages.
But when the penance
ended, his sight
flew out
into the open sky
and over the fields,
innocently coming
to rest on each self-
expressing element
of creation
with such delight
and gratitude
he couldn't keep
the words from
pouring out of him.

VISION

I just got back from the eye doctor, who told me
I need bifocals. She put those drops in my eyes
that dilate the pupils, so everything has
that vaseline-on-the-lens glow around it,
and the page I'm writing on is blurred
and blinding, even with these sunglasses.
I'm waiting for the "reversing drops" to kick in
(sounds like something from *Alice in Wonderland*),
but meanwhile I like the way our golden retriever
looks more golden than ever, the way the black-eyed
Susans seem to break out of their contours, dilating
into some semi-visionary version of themselves,
and even the mail truck emanates a white light
as if it might be delivering news so good
I can't even imagine it. Of course it's just bills,
catalogues, and an issue of *Time* magazine
full of pictures of a flooded New Orleans
that I have to hold at arm's length to make out:
a twisted old woman sprouting plastic tubes
lies with others on an airport conveyor belt
like unclaimed luggage, and there's a woman feeding
her dog on an overpass as a body floats below.
Maybe we need some kind of bifocals
to take it all in—the darkness and the light,
our own lives and the lives of others, suffering
and joy, if it is out there—or something more
like the compound eyes of these crimson dragonflies
patrolling the yard, each lens focused on some
different facet of reality, and linked to a separate
part of the brain. We would probably go crazy.
In my own eyes with their single, flawed lenses,
the drops have almost worn off now, and my pupils
are narrowing down, adjusting themselves
to their diminished vision of the world.

Afterword

The maple limb severed
by a December storm
still blossoms in May
where it lies on the ground,

its red tassels a message
from the other side,
like a letter arriving
after its writer has died.

II

TO A SNAKE

I knew you were not poisonous
when I saw you in the side garden;
even your name—milk snake—
sounds harmless, and yet your pattern
of copper splotches outlined in black
frightened me, and the way you were
curled in loops; and it offended me
that you were so close to the house
and clearly living underneath it
if not inside, in the cellar, where I
have found your torn shed skins.

You must have been frightened too
when I caught you in the webbing
of the lacrosse stick and flung you
into the woods, where you landed
dangling from a vine-covered branch,
shamelessly twisted. Now I
am the one who is ashamed, unable
to untangle my feelings,
braided into my DNA or buried
deep in the part of my brain
that is most like yours.

Natural History of the Yard

All spring I'd been playing hide-and-seek
with the groundhog living under the shed,
looking out for it when I went in or out
of the house, peeking from behind the garage
or sitting quietly reading in a lawn chair
until it poked its head out tentatively
then ventured farther by degrees to munch
my weedy lawn or just lounge in the sun,
our common pleasure. Its roguishness amused me,
as did the way it bolted toward the shed,
revealing the russet fur of its outstretched legs.

How different (though about the same size)
was the giant snapping turtle I saw one day
mechanically high-stepping across the yard,
its thick, uncircumcised head extended menacingly
and spined tail, like a Bronze Age weapon,
stabbing out from under the cataphracted shell.
It elevated itself on fat stubby legs
as I approached, then slowly bore itself
like an armored vehicle into the woods,
returning to its separate world, ancient
but somehow concurrent with our own.

But the groundhog, or groundhogs—because now
there were two—were our warm-blooded tenants.
So I was glad at first when a young one
appeared on the lawn. But something was wrong:
it hauled itself pathetically through the grass,
dragging its back legs behind, their dark, rubbery
underpaws upturned, like useless flippers.
Not long for this world, I thought, as I coaxed it
nevertheless back toward the shed, thinking again

of the snapper, of its barbed jaw clamping down,
unable to keep myself from taking sides.

Parts of an Old House

I. Pump

Before the screened porch was glassed in
to become a TV room, and the chest full of kindling
and pile of split logs that shrank and grew
were replaced by a sofa and coffee table,
the old pump of rusted iron stood like a relic,
though we still used it to fill the dog's bowl
or a watering can, or a bucket for some chore
(there were still chores then)—or just for fun,

grabbing the long curving handle and pumping it
hard, three or four times, before the water
started streaming out of the fat spout
in a coarse rope. It wasn't the same water
that came out of the faucets in the house
but rainwater that collected in a cistern
underground, our father explained. It tasted of rust
and old leaves, though we weren't supposed to drink it.

And then one day when we got home from school,
it lay beside the driveway, the long pipe that had extended
into the ground unseen trailing behind it,
badly bent—a vulnerable thing,
its magic gone, disconnected I sensed even then
from a whole era, as it was from the cistern ...
which is still there, under the earth, full of dark water
I would taste again now if I could.

2. Smokehouse

Brick painted white on the outside, and inside
blackened by smoke, windowless, it stood
in the driveway's circle as if central to our lives
and not, as even in childhood we knew,
the vestige of a long-gone epoch, antebellum,
now used only for storing rusty bicycles,
old grills, tires worn smooth, chipped flower pots,
bird feeders, shovels, rakes with bent prongs,
red dented gas cans, green hoses coiled like snakes.

It scared my brothers and me to unlatch the door
that was one shade darker than the yews that flanked it
and grew shaggier, taller, and more shadowy each year,
but one time, playing hide-and-seek, I crept
into that dim cell smelling of dank ash,
cool even in summer, like a mausoleum,
and hung with (as my eyes adjusted) cobwebs,
wasp nests, and tattered snakeskins—shivering,
heart pounding, praying to be found.

3. Banister

The railing along the upstairs hallway made a
hairpin turn and angled down into the word
banister, which sounded grand and meant something
that grown-ups steadied themselves with, but for us boys
was for sliding down: we mounted it like a horse,
feeling giddy from the height and holding tight,
then loosened our grip to let ourselves slip down
backwards, the skin of our damp palms squeaking
along its varnished length and burning a little
as we squeezed again to stop ourselves at the bottom.

Soon it became second nature: I hardly gave it
any thought as I swung my leg over
to transport myself from upstairs to down
how many times a day ... just as we hardly noticed,
as we grew older, that we'd stopped, our attention
drawn elsewhere, the banister becoming something
that we absently passed our hands over,
or that just ran unnoticed alongside us
as we came and went and finally left that house
entirely for college and the rest of our lives.

We must have assumed that everything
would just keep sliding along smoothly,
as though the banister had followed us right out
the door and was still there next to us
like a rail invisibly guiding us along.
Of course, we were wrong. There were times
when we stumbled, and one of us lost
his balance utterly, and the rest of us felt
the sudden need to reach out and grip
something solid, only to find nothing there.

DANGER: TULIPS

Hoping to find my way to the river, wide
with April's rain, and to see, perhaps,
a few wildflowers, and maybe a cardinal
whistling in a blossoming tree, I took a path
I'd never taken before, first through woods
then up a sloping meadow, above whose green rise
appeared, with each step, first the slate roofs
and then the red brick walls of what I realized
was the abandoned state mental hospital.

My instinct was to turn away, but something drew me
toward those old buildings, each marked on the door
with a red X to show it was condemned.
The plywood filling the windows, painted red,
didn't keep me from imagining the scenes
that must have happened behind them.
So it was with relief that I saw the church
with its brick bell-tower and mostly intact
stained glass, and made my way toward it.

I tried the door then noticed the red plaque
engraved with *cancer* and *asbestos*,
and backed away. I wanted to get out of there,
to wash that place's toxins from my skin.
But circling around back, I found a garden
thick with weeds yet blooming nevertheless,
as it always had each spring,
with daffodils and purple hyacinths
and the reddest tulips I had ever seen.

The Figure on the Hill

When I saw the figure on the crown of the hill,
high above the city, standing perfectly still

against a sky so saturated with the late-
afternoon, late-summer Pacific light

that granules of it seemed to have come out
of solution, like a fine precipitate

of crystals hanging in the brightened air,
I thought whoever it was standing up there

must be experiencing some heightened state
of being, or thinking—or its opposite,

thoughtlessly enraptured by the view.
Or maybe, looking again, it was a statue

of Jesus or a saint, placed there to bestow
a ceaseless blessing on the city below.

Only after a good five minutes did I see
that the figure was actually a tree—

some kind of cypress, probably, or cedar.
I was both amused and let down by my error.

Not only had I made the tree a person,
but I'd also given it a vision,

which seemed to linger in the light-charged air
around the tree's green flame, then disappear.

The Day You Looked upon Me as a Stranger,

I had left you at the gate to buy a newspaper
and on my way back stopped at a bank of monitors
to check the status of our flight to London.

That was when you noticed a middle-aged man
in a brown jacket and the green short-brimmed cap
I'd bought for the trip. It wasn't until I turned

and walked toward you that you saw him as me.
What a nice-looking man, you told me you'd thought—
maybe European, with that unusual cap ...

somebody, you said, you might want to meet.
We both laughed. And it aroused my vanity
that you had been attracted to me afresh,

with no baggage. A kind of affirmation.
But doubt seeped into that crevice of time
when you had looked upon me as a stranger,

and I wondered if you'd pictured him
as someone more intriguing than I could be
after decades of marriage, all my foibles known.

Did you have one of those under-the-radar daydreams
of meeting him, hitting it off, and getting
on a plane together? In those few moments,

did you imagine a whole life with him?
And were you disappointed, or glad, to find
it was only the life you already had?

SLIP

If I call my son by my daughter's name
or vice versa; or if I call one of them
by the dog's name, or the other way around—
all of which I have been known to do—
it's funny, and only means I'm spaced out.

But when, while talking on my cell phone,
I walked past my new African American colleague
and distractedly said hi, using the name
of another black colleague, it was stupendously
unfunny. I felt like I'd been punched

in the stomach, which is probably what
I deserved, even if he shrugged it off,
as he seemed to do when I caught up with him
and apologized too fervently,
my assumption that I'd caused him pain

itself a kind of racism, no doubt. It's so
complicated!—though it doesn't seem to be
for my teenage son and daughter,
and I'm glad of that, and admire their ease.
As for me and my colleague that day,

he absolved me with offhand grace,
doing his best to nudge me away
from my floundering shame, then
gently steered the conversation elsewhere
the way one does to protect a child.

Remembering Karenia Brevis

Coughing, my eyes and nostrils burning,
I read in the local paper that the red tide
is caused by an algae called Karenia Brevis,

a name like that of a girl in high school,
the one all the boys had a crush on
but who seemed to inhabit a medium

they couldn't breathe. She had red hair, of course,
a blaze of it that spread a conflagration
in the tangled underbrush of their brains.

But her eyes were a cool green, like the shallow
stretches of a tropical sea—say, in Boca Grande
where her family vacationed every spring.

Unpredictable, not fully understood,
susceptible to mysterious currents,
it was as though she emitted a toxin

that paralyzed the lungs and vocal cords
of nerds and jocks alike, who swooned around her
like the sheepshead, blowfish, mullets, and snook

that have been washing up on shore
these past few weeks, or the Goliath grouper
I saw yesterday, sprawled in the sand,

at first mistaking it for a grown man.

Magatama

When I saw it there among the tide's crushed shells—
a small, gray-green stone worn by the green ocean
into a smooth curve shaped like a comma,
or like a primitive creature, all head and tail,
staring up at me with its one round eye, a hole
bored through by the elements exactly where
you'd drill a hole to thread a cord through
to wear it as a pendant—I already knew
that was what I would do, and I picked it up
and held it out to show my son and daughter,
uttering the funny word *magatama.*

It had only been a few weeks earlier,
that my friend Charlie, who lives in Japan,
told me about magatamas: curved beads
of agate or jade, now sold as amulets,
but whose origins go back so far
that their religious meanings are uncertain—
an apt emblem, I thought, for my own uncertain
religious impulses, so I asked him to buy me one.
Which he did, saying this was the first gem
he had ever purchased for any man
or woman. He would mail it soon.

But now I'd found another magatama, not of jade,
but made and given to me by the ocean itself.
And immediately I became afraid
that I would lose it, so I put it in my mouth,
the salt on its small hard tongue dissolving
on my tongue, its stoniness tapping against
the stoniness of my teeth as I began to sing
a nonsense song (my children laughing at me
for acting like a child), singing the song

of the magatama with the magatama
in my very mouth singing the song.

A week later, the envelope arrived,
flimsy blue airmail paper whose folded edge
had worn through, or been slit: the magatama
had either been stolen or fallen out.
So I would not have that polished magatama
from my closest friend who lives far away,
but instead this unlikely one that intervened,
slipping through the slit crease of some other-
worldly envelope, or at least through the worn edge
of the jade-green sea, happening to be just there
at the instant my eyes had fallen to find it.

ENOUGH

It's a gift, this cloudless November morning
warm enough to walk without a jacket
along your favorite path. The rhythmic shushing
of your feet through fallen leaves should be
enough to quiet the mind, so it surprises you
when you catch yourself telling off your boss
for a decade of accumulated injustices,
all the things you've never said circling inside you.

The rising wind pulls you out of it,
and you look up to see a cloud of leaves
wheeling in sunlight, flickering against the blue
and lifting above the treetops, as if the whole day
were sighing, *Let it go, let it go,*
for this moment at least, let it all go.

Ivan Ilyich at the Lake

When the dragonfly landed on my book,
I was drifting on the lake in a kayak
reading Tolstoy's "The Death of Ivan Ilyich"
in a paperback so old that each yellowed page
came loose with a tiny cracking sound
as I turned it—the book itself as deciduous
as the maples on shore, which had started to turn.
I was fifty, and naturally the story
had led to thoughts about how false or true
my life had been, to all the ways
I was and was not like Ivan Ilyich.
To think that I had failed at everything
he had succeeded at—money, status,
connections, an impressive beard—seemed
only self-congratulatory. I had my own
sins and shortcomings, which I avoided
with my own evasive maneuvers.

I was just going back to the story when
the dragonfly appeared, like an answer
that refused to answer other than with
itself, seeming to ask nothing of me but that I
look carefully through my reading glasses
at the intricate veined structure of its wings,
the mineral sheen of its out-of-proportion eyes,
and its long, thin, segmented tail of gasflame blue
that pulsed above the still-fastened page.
I was grateful for the quick gift of its visit,
but I saw that it too might be only
a diversion, a way to avoid looking hard
at myself—and just then it took off
with a sudden snapping flutter of its wings
and darted away in erratic flight,

leaving me to return to Ilyich's death,
the blue lake shimmering all around me.

III

AFTER READING HAN SHAN

I like to climb the local mountain—
actually, just a hill with a rocky peak—
so that, when my arm is extended,
the city some twenty miles away
takes up the space of about an inch
between my forefinger and thumb.

Of the people who work in those tiny
skyscrapers, whose year-end bonuses
are more than I make in ten years of teaching,
I ask: Are they any more alive than I am?
And, a hundred years from now,
will they be any less dead?

My dog sniffing among the boulders
is unconcerned with such questions
and pays no attention to the view.
Distances of time and space
are tricks of the mind. What matters
is what's happening under your nose.

But I am not a dog. When I go down the hill,
I'll be right back in the world again.
Which may be why I like the way
everything between the city and me
seems to be trees, no roads or houses visible,
nothing, from here to there, but shades of green.

WORK

I'm sitting at the kitchen table, working
on a poem, though that locution might amuse
the carpenter and his two assistants
who are in the basement and driveway
attending to the rotting bulkhead frame
and replacing a cellar window so far gone
I could stick my thumb right into the sill.
A small job, but still a day's actual work,
maybe two. I hear them calling measurements,
the shriek of the circular saw, a hammer
banging just under my feet, a loud, grinding
vibration that comes from I don't know what
infernal tool, an occasional laugh
revealing the play in their work. And here
is where I could begin maneuvering
into an analogy between carpentry
and the making of poems, hauling in
the whole vocabulary of woodworking:
level, plumb, dovetail, and especially *true.*
But that poem has already been written
more than once, and it would ignore
the undercurrent of uselessness I feel
sitting at the kitchen table doing what
any respectable carpenter would call
nothing. And if that undercurrent is
one of the hazards of the job, it's nothing
compared to what could be done to a thumb
with a circular saw. Plus, they seem
much better than I am at getting things right
the first time. The poem I was working on
before I started this one, and which I've been
working on for several months, on and off,
is about pine trees, which is funny because

I'm sure the boards these guys are using
are pine. Not that they wouldn't understand
or even appreciate my attempts to get at
the druidical otherness of the trees
or enjoy this poem that is partly about them.

But even if either poem were finished,
I probably wouldn't be taking it with me
when I go out to chat with them as they eat lunch.
I don't even point out the pines themselves,
rising above the woods not fifty yards
from where they sit on the tailgate of their truck.
They laugh at my dog eating sawdust
and ask his name. We talk about the Red Sox.
Their work looks good, and I tell them so.

POEM

I'm going to pretend I'm a painter and just
set up my easel here in the tall grass
by the river, with the bridge in the distance,
because the bridge needs to be in the picture
with its steel trusses and concrete pylons
streaked with rust, something to give structure,
something man-made, a work of art
or at least of engineering to connect
not only the two banks of the river but also
the earth to the sky, fastening them
together like a row of thick stitches.

If I were really a painter I wouldn't have to
say all that but just paint the damn bridge,
freed from the smeary imprecision and duplicity
of words, though I could still make the bridge
look like stitches by painting it black
against a sunset's bloody wound—but that
would be its own kind of falsity, so maybe
it's only an illusion that a different
medium would connect me more directly
to the world, and the wound may be
inside me anyway, and these the stitches.

Listening to Virginia

Virginia Leishman reading To the Lighthouse

Driving around town doing errands,
I almost have to pull to the side of the road
because I can't go on another minute without
seeing the words of some gorgeous passage
in the paperback I keep on the passenger seat . . .
but I resist that impulse and keep listening,
until it is almost Woolf herself sitting beside me
like some dear great aunt who happens to be a genius
telling me stories in a voice like sparkling waves
and following eddies of thought into the minds
of other people sitting around a dinner table
or strolling under the trees, pulling me along
in the current of her words like a twig riding a stream
around boulders and down foaming cascades,
getting drawn into a whirlpool of consciousness
and sucked under swirling into the thoughts of
someone else, swimming for a time among the reeds
and glinting minnows before breaking free
and popping back up to the surface only to discover
that in my engrossment I've overshot
the grocery store and have to turn around,
and even after I'm settled in the parking lot
I can't stop but sit there with the car idling
because now she is going over it all again
though differently this time, with new details
or from inside the mind of someone else,
as if each person were a hive, with its own
murmurs and stirrings, that we visit like bees,
haunting its dark compartments, but reaching
only so far, never to the very heart, the queen's
chamber where the deepest secrets are stored
(and only there to truly know another person),

though the vibrations and the dance of the worker bees
tell us something, give us something we can take
with us as we fly back out into honeyed daylight.

The Digestive Fallacy

*"There is the strong instinct in me which I cannot analyse—to draw
and describe the things I love . . . a sort of instinct like that for eating or
drinking. I should like to draw all St. Marks . . . stone by stone—to eat
it all up into my mind—touch by touch."*
　　　　　　　　　　　　　　　　—John Ruskin, in a letter, 1852

He wanted to eat San Marco, stone
by stone, to savor, like confections,
the palazzi along the Grand Canal,
and spoon up their melting reflections—

all through the act of drawing,
or painting them with words.
And not just foreign places,
but shells or the feathers of birds.

And Rose La Touche, who was ten
when he first saw her, nude on a dune—
to touch that untouchable skin,
he drew her again and again.

He wanted to bottle the English skies
and keep them on a pantry shelf
like a collection of fine sherries
to which he'd later treat himself;

he described their textures and colors
and their psychological effects
until the labels grew so large
the bottles were wrapped in texts.

But that hardly mattered: the point
was to take in what went unnoticed,
to praise the world—not fame,
not to become an artist.

On Bitching

after Catullus

Listen, Hilarius, you've got to snap out of it.
I know you're in your fifties now,
but don't let yourself give in to bitterness.
Sure, when you were younger the muse
used to visit more often, sprawling across your lap
and whispering in your ear, but at least
she treats you now and then to an idea
or plants a stanza in your head as you're waking up.
And stop bitching about editors
who keep publishing each other's poems
in *Pretension Quarterly* or *The Moribund Review*.
Why waste your energy enumerating
all the petty injustices that have gone on
since ancient times and are bound to continue
for centuries to come? And there's no point
in envying the poets who swagger into rooms,
charging every molecule with their need
to be important. So, let them be important.
And if, sometimes, you feel as if you
hardly exist, well, as a great poet once said,
be secret and exult … instead of sulking.
Believe me, I agree with you, it's too bad
things sometimes work the way they do,
but it's exasperating to listen to you
after you've had a few too many cups of wine
railing against the zealously self-promoting
postmodern obfuscators, the hip ironists revved up
on their own cleverness, the tedious fundamentalists
of rhyme and meter, or the one you call
the formalist narcissist Stalinist surrealist.
Not bad, Hilarius, but you need to get over it.
You didn't want power, remember?

You wanted to write poems. So, write them.
And the next time some self-satisfied preener
wins a prize, don't dwell on it, but remind yourself
of all the poems that didn't get away, the poems
of your friends and how they've borne you up
and spurred you on with a better envy,
and remember the friends themselves, laboring
alone at their desks, mostly under the radar
(unlike the "famous poets" you call the oxymorons),
and giving you what literary life you have
which if not dazzling is at least genuine—
and thank the gods to the end of your days
for the time they've granted you to spend
on making poems, even if they come to nothing.

Roofer

Amazing that the roofer who comes over
to check our lichened shingles turns out to be
a poet—a slam poet, actually. Long-haired,
thirty-five-ish, in ripped jeans, he looks
like someone who could sound his "barbaric yawp
over the roofs of the world"—over them and *from* them—
though it seems he's pretty much given up poetry
to pursue his trade. He's as surprised
as I am to have found another poet,
and we engage in some animated shoptalk,
even touching on a local poet whose success
we gripe about, before returning to the subject
of my roof. He climbs his ladder, looks around,
then comes back down. "It's brittle," he says,
"but not a complete disaster ... unlike the poems
of that asshole we were talking about." I laugh.
Before he leaves, I give him one of my books.

Afterwards, I wonder if I should have
learned a trade, one of the occupations
Whitman celebrated, in which one can find
(I have to look it up) "the eternal meanings"
and "all themes, hints, possibilities."
Not to mention a good living, judging by
the ballpark estimate the roofer gave me.
He's going to write it up and send it to me,
along with—who knows?—a critique of my poems
("Turn up the volume!") or a sheaf of his own,
which I imagine to be enviably charged
with a giddy urgency, as if shouted
from a steeply pitched roof.
And isn't a book of poems, when placed
face down on a table, to hold one's page,

something like a gable, a small roof
of paper and words, a place to dwell?

RENEWAL

At the Department of Motor Vehicles
to renew my driver's license, I had to wait
two hours on one of those wooden benches
like pews in the Church of Latter Day
Meaninglessness, where there is no
stained glass (no windows at all, in fact),
no incense other than stale cigarette smoke
emanating from the clothes of those around me,
and no sermon, just an automated female voice
calling numbers over a loudspeaker.
And one by one the members of our sorry
congregation shuffled meekly up to the pitted
altar to have our vision tested or to seek
redemption for whatever wrong turn we'd taken,
or pay indulgences, or else be turned away
as unworthy of piloting our own journey.
But when I paused to look around, using my numbered
ticket as a bookmark, it was as if the dim
fluorescent light had been transformed
to incandescence. The face of the Latino guy
in a ripped black sweatshirt glowed with health,
and I could tell that the sulking white girl
accompanied by her mother was brimming
with secret excitement to be getting her first license,
already speeding down the highway, alone,
with all the windows open, singing.

Commuter Buddhist

I'm learning to be a Buddhist in my car,
listening to a book on tape. One problem
is that, before I've gotten very far,

my mind gradually becomes aware
that it has stopped listening, straying from
the task of becoming a Buddhist in my car.

I'm also worried that listening will impair
my driving, as the package label cautions,
but I haven't noticed that, at least so far.

In fact, I may be driving with more care.
There's a sensation of attentive calm
that's part of becoming a Buddhist in your car.

A soothing voice drones on until the car
is transformed into a capsule of wisdom
traveling at high speed, and you feel far

from anywhere but where you really are . . .
which is nowhere, really. The biggest problem
is getting the Buddhism *out* of your car
and into your life. I've failed at that so far.

The Day Nothing Happened

*"British computer scientists have determined that April 11, 1954, was
the most boring day of the twentieth century."*   —*news item*

On that day in history, history
took a day off. Current events
were uneventful. Breaking news
never broke. Nobody
of any import was born, or died.
(If you were born that day,
bask in the inverted glory
of your unimportance.)
No milestones, no disasters.
The most significant thing going on
was a golf tournament (the Masters).

It was a Sunday. In Washington,
President Eisenhower
(whose very name induces sleep)
practiced his putt
on the carpet of the Oval Office,
a little white ball crossing
and recrossing the presidential seal
like one of Jupiter's moons
or a hypnotist's watch.
On the radio, Perry Como
was putting everyone into a coma.

But the very next day,
in New York City,
Bill Haley & His Comets
recorded "Rock Around the Clock,"
and a few young people
began to regain consciousness...
while history, like Polyphemus

waking from a one-day slumber,
stumbled out of his cave,
blinked his giant eye, and peered around
for something to destroy.

THE SHOULDERS OF WOMEN

Bored by the featureless speeches at the fundraising dinner,
I scan the hotel ballroom for something to look at
and discover (thank God for sleeveless dresses!)
the shoulders of women, pale moons aglow
above the linen-covered tables. Smooth and rounded
like the neighboring breasts, they are less obvious
and more complex, their inner mechanism
of muscle, tendon, cartilage, and bone
giving detail and highlights to their contours,
making more exquisite the way the skin
is pulled taut across the clavicle's diagonal ridge
then dips into that shallow well above it,
the way it curves down, then up again unseen
into the nether hollow of the underarm,
that tender pocket, the shoulder's hidden nest.
The speaker patters on about how there has never
been a more important time than now, and I
have to agree, because when will I ever see
a collection of shoulders as marvelous as this?
I feel blessed to have been let in on this
open secret: all over the room, women revealing
the rounded upper corners of their nakedness.
And when the speeches finally end, I applaud
not for what was said, but for these women,
for the shoulders they have so generously given.

ALICE NEEL'S SOIRÉE

after an Alice Neel exhibition

She greets us at the top of the stairs,
not nude but naked, her flesh
bulking forward as she heaves
herself up from the striped chair.
Her cheeks are pink but she's not blushing.
Unashamed of her Mother Hubbard body,
she looks right at us through
the only thing she's wearing (glasses)
as she invites us to take off our clothes.

We feel a little square for not complying
until we see that most of the other guests
are dressed, although a good third
are wandering around in the buff,
including a bemused and foul-smelling fellow
who seems to have a couple of extra
penises strapped to his pelvis
and claims to be writing an oral
history of the universe.

It's an odd mix: curators, artists, family,
neighbors, street people, transvestites,
and one Fuller Brush man with a boyish
chipmunky look, whose blue bow tie
matches his eyes. He's got a few samples
in his breast pocket, and as he pulls one out
I notice the numbers tattooed to his wrist.
Nearby, someone clearly crazy, with scarlet ears,
writhes in an armchair, snarling. I give him

a wide berth. There are a few big names: Warhol
appears to be meditating with his shirt off,
his serene expression a sharp

contrast with the long scars that crisscross
his abdomen below his woman's breasts.
There's Meyer Schapiro, wrinkled down
to his eyelids but still lively. And there's
the porn star Annie Sprinkle, sporting,
among other accoutrements, a padlock in her vagina.

I hear someone say Allen Ginsberg
might show up. Meanwhile, I keep
almost recognizing people then blurting
the wrong names, but most of them
don't seem to mind—except for one,
a curator from the Met, who gets bitchy
when I ask if he's Truman Capote.
The Wall Street tycoon (face shadowed with green)
looks a little like Harold Bloom.

Alice waddles through the room, holding
a paintbrush like a wand, or as if
she were the nonchalant conductor
of this human symphony.
She's put on a blue dress: "I was beginning
to feel like so much meat," she says
to a woman wearing nothing
but a huge blue hat and pink panties.
"But you of course are a glorious creature."

Then I see Frank O'Hara from across the room,
his nose in profile like a small cliff, unmistakable,
his eyes wide in a blue trance and the lilacs
behind him seeming to crown his head,
and I rush over to him as to an old friend
and tell him how much I've always wanted to meet him,
and when he turns toward me I'm not sure
if he's smiling or grimacing until he says,
"Well, what on earth has taken you so long?"

THE GENERATIONS

Years from now I may have forgotten all
the details, so I'm trying to get this down
on paper now in order to have it then
when I'm old and looking back on that evening
of the poetry festival's last day when
Wilbur and Snodgrass and Strand were all
in one room for what might be the last time,
with a slew of us likely to be forgotten
sitting around that living room or standing
along its bookshelved walls and in the doorways,
listening to toasts and then to our spirited host
intoning Yeats's "Sailing to Byzantium."
Then we heard Wyatt, Herrick, Bishop, Larkin,
and I'm already forgetting who else,
nursery rhymes in English and Hungarian,
all by heart from those in our gathering,
poem after poem called back and delivered
and listened to with the insuppressible pleasure
of poets celebrating the art of those who came
centuries or decades before them.
I can't remember, already, who asked for Wilbur's
"Love Calls Us to the Things of This World."
He said he couldn't do it from memory,
and someone handed him the book. As he read it
from his armchair, I could see Strand, standing
behind him, on the far side of the room,
mouthing the words as if they were a creed—
then he backed away, though I could see him still
from my corner as he bent his head forward
and covered his face with his hands. For a moment
I thought he was overcome with emotion,
and maybe, for a moment, he was—at the poem
itself, and from remembering the time
(from the vantage of now being seventy-three)

he'd memorized those lines by his elder.
And not just those lines, because, moments later,
he stepped forward to recite another poem
by Wilbur, following it with a parody
he'd written in college, then placed his hand
on Wilbur's shoulder to show him it was meant
in further homage. And I felt how rare it was,
this paying tribute, this camaraderie,
this sense of being however small a part
of something much larger than that room.

IV

LIGHT SNOW

Just enough snow fell last night
to emphasize what's there—nothing
fanciful, no octopi on the spruce boughs
or fungal protuberances in the garden—
just enough to highlight the cables
swooping in unison above the road
and to italicize the branches of the trees
out to their twiggy extremities
so that their complex articulations
might be legible. But what is it
I want to read in them? Just enough
to see what's there a little more clearly?
Or a little more than that? I don't know,
but what I see next is the snow
being blown from the trees in sudden
glittering puffs, one after another
of these literal illuminations
that swirl down and vanish,
dazzling, ungraspable.

Out Walking

"The late year has grown fresh again and new
As Spring ... "

I took a walk with Edward Thomas
across the hills of Gloucestershire,
still green in mild late December,
the Sunday before Christmas.

His language as fresh as water,
as clear as birdsong or the bells
that drifted up from a village,
was what I seemed to need that day;

and I liked the way he pointed out
with quiet enthusiasm
a bird's nest wreathed into a hedge
or a wildflower still in bloom.

The beaters pacing a muddy field
of turnips, cracking their white flags
to flush partridges and pheasants
over a grove where hunters hid,

turned our talk to distant wars.
We heard faint shots and saw birds drop,
and cheered the ones that made it through,
winging their way to farther fields.

That was where we headed, too,
"nearly regardless of footpaths,"
getting lost to make a game
of finding our way back again.

"Pure earth and wind and sunlight"
were the elements he said he loved.
Then he grew quiet, as though to become
"nothing but breathing and seeing,"

and by the time I took the lane
back into town, I was alone,
though in the pocket of my coat
my hand still held his book of poems.

SHAKING OFF THE SNOW

The snow was heavy and clung thickly to the trees,
and there was no sun yet to start it melting
and give them some relief. Some trees had cracked,
others bowed in fringed arcs over the trail,
and some bent so low they blocked the trail entirely.
I shook one off and watched it spring back up
and laughed as it dumped snow on me,
and on the snow-covered ground with muffled thunder.

Then I kept following the closed-in trail
and opening it up, shaking the trees
and letting them go, and showering myself with snow.
The branches that sometimes whipped me in the face
and the clumps of snow stinging my neck and forehead
were a price worth paying to see the trees fly up.
One pulled my glove right off, a woolen leaf.
One good-sized oak almost lifted me off the ground.

I thought of Frost's birches, lifting the boy up,
and of his crow that shook snow down on him,
changing his mood. It seemed I needed more
than just a dusting. I needed to be covered
from head to toe. And I couldn't get enough
of the bowed-over trees springing back up.
By the end, I was soaked, sweating under my clothes,
almost happy, my pockets filled with snow.

NEST

Not until we got the Christmas tree
into the house and up on the stand
did our daughter discover a small bird's nest
tucked among its needled branches.

Amazing, that the nest had made it
all the way from Nova Scotia on a truck
mashed together with hundreds of other trees
without being dislodged or crushed.

And now it made the tree feel wilder,
a balsam fir growing in our living room,
as though at any moment a bird might flutter
through the house and return to the nest.

Yet because we'd brought the tree indoors,
we'd turned the nest into the first ornament.
So we wound the tree with strings of lights,
draped it with strands of red beads,

and added the other ornaments, then dropped
two small brass bells into the nest, like eggs
containing music, and hung a painted goldfinch
from the branch above, as if to keep them warm.

MAILBOXES IN LATE WINTER

What a motley lot. A few still stand
at attention like sentries at the ends
of their driveways, but more lean
askance as if they'd just received a blow
to the head, and in fact they've received
many, all winter, from jets of wet snow
shooting off the curved, tapered blade
of the plow. Some look wobbly, cocked
at oddball angles or slumping forlornly
on precariously listing posts. One box
bows steeply forward, as if in disgrace, its door
lolling sideways, unhinged. Others are dented,
battered, streaked with rust, bandaged in duct tape,
crisscrossed with clothesline or bungee cords.
A few lie abashed in remnants of the very snow
that knocked them from their perches.
Another is wedged in the crook of a tree
like a birdhouse, its post shattered nearby.
I almost feel sorry for them, worn out
by the long winter, off-kilter, not knowing
what hit them, trying to hold themselves
together, as they wait for news from spring.

CREATURE COMFORTS

It's a snow day for us, but not
for the kids, so after they're off
to school, we jump back in bed
to make love, allowing ourselves
to let out the whimpers and moans
we usually suppress in our tiny
house where everything can be heard.
But as we're going at it, we hear
faint steps on the stairs and hold still
for a breathless moment, then realize
it's the dog, curious about the strange
sounds his keen ears have picked up.
He pads into the bedroom and stares
at us moving under the check quilt,
head cocked, a canine voyeur—
though, poor neutered creature, he doesn't
understand what he's looking at.
Or does he? Now *he* is whimpering
and we're laughing, saying his name
to reassure him as we keep going,
right in front of him, unashamed,
in dogged pursuit of our animal pleasure.

You Don't Put Flowers in Poems

You don't put flowers in poems
for decoration, or to fill in
empty spaces, but because
they punctuated your days
at a certain juncture—
like the milkweed blooming
by the road when I went running
(sweating and thinking about sex)
that first summer we were apart,
the first year we were together.
I pressed one sweet pink globe
between the pages of my Rimbaud
and enclosed it with a letter.
Thirty-two years later,
its stain still marks the poems.

ISLAND, 1979

For a week we slept on the least accessible beach
in a single sleeping bag, or on top of it,
spreading it out on the black volcanic sand.
We swam in the blue Aegean, lounged in the sun
and in the shade of small pines, read books (mine
was incongruously *Crime and Punishment*),
made love, and took turns noodling on a little flute
a friend had given us. Every morning we walked
into the village of white houses with blue doors
and bought fresh bread and ripe tomatoes,
slicing both with my Swiss Army knife.
We subsisted on tomato sandwiches
and on each other. We never even bothered
with the ancient ruins, or the famous nightlife
we heard about later, never explored the island,
didn't feel the need to make sure we weren't
missing anything. There was nothing missing,
except maybe protein. Not that it was perfect:
you sunbathed topless for the first and last time
and scorched your breasts, and we did get tired
of tomatoes and that same bread every meal.
Still, it was a week worthy of holding dear
thirty years later, an island of time as remote
as the real one, never to be returned to,
and we don't even have any photographs
to show we were there or prove to our teenagers
that we were once almost as young as them ...
though I do remember one we used to have
of you, beautifully sun-browned in your maroon
bathing suit, playing the flute under a pine.
And I have a picture in my mind of the green
Indian-print dress you wore all that summer
and looked so good in. Long gone now,

as is the bathing suit. We still have the sleeping bag
but not the flute. And I don't know what became
of the paperback *I Ching* we'd picked up in Athens,
and which we consulted, flipping drachmas,
to figure out which day we'd leave the island.

TEMPLE

Not a place of worship exactly
but one I like to go back to
and where, you could say, I take
sanctuary: this smooth area
above the ear and around the corner
from your forehead, where your hair
is as silky as milkweed.
The way to feel its featheriness best
is with the lips. Though you
are going gray, right there
your hair is as soft as a girl's,
the two of us briefly young again
when I kiss your temple.

Brief Note for April's Departure

Since you will be leaving
tomorrow (or actually tonight,
just after midnight),
I wanted to jot a few words to you
while I still have the chance,
and not simply to repeat
the common accusation of cruelty,
though the way you are warm
for a week then suddenly
cold again does seem unkind,
and it is sometimes hard
not to resent those friends
who lead us on with sunny smiles
only to withhold their feelings
or parcel them out leaf
by leaf, as if saving them
for others, elsewhere.

But perhaps you were just waiting
for the right moment to open
up to us, the delay teetering
between heightening delight
and simply coming too late . . .
until finally you gave us crocuses
pecking out of the earth's shell,
the rabbit ears of daffodils
and their self-trumpeting flowers,
forsythia going haywire
in electric yellow, then leaves
in amazing miniature
like the fingers of infants,
and coiled ferns beginning
their slow unfurling—enough

so that we start to miss you
just before you leave.

Nobody Died

How many times did I say it
over the past decade,
until it became a kind of mantra,
the measure of any crisis:
"Nobody died."

I said it to myself
to put events in perspective,
and I said it to others
to remind them that things
could be worse.

Always in the background
was the awful fact
of my brother's death;
for any lesser calamity
I needed to be grateful.

Our house was burglarized:
diamond earrings, pearl necklaces,
all handed down
by ancestors long dead.
"Nobody died," I said.

It was like a charm
I wore around my neck
as a form of protection,
an evil eye
to stare down death.

I said it again
to our friends at the lake
when their boathouse burned down,

but felt how selfish I was
to be ranking their misfortune.

And then the phrase began
to go sour. I worried
that it might be asking for trouble
to keep saying, "Nobody died,"
a way of taunting death.

So I quietly let it go,
as if to row out
far from shore
and drop the amulet
into the lake's all-seeing eye.

THE SAME RIVER

Yes, yes, you can't step into the same
river twice, but all the same, this river
is one of the things that has changed
least in my life, and stepping into it
always feels like returning to something
far back and familiar, its steady current
of coppery water flowing around my calves
and then my thighs, my only waders
a pair of old shorts. Holding a fly rod
above my head, my other arm out
for balance, like some kind of dance,
trying not to slip on the mossy rocks,
I make my way out to the big rock
I want to fish from, mottled with lichen
that has dried to rusty orange, a small
midstream island that a philosopher
might use to represent *stasis*
versus *flux*, *being* amidst *becoming*,
in some argument that is larger
than any that interests me now
as I climb out dripping onto the boulder
and cast my line out to where the bubbles
form a channel and trail off in a V
that points to where the fish might be,
holding steady amid the river's flow.

A Drink of Water

When my nineteen-year-old son turns on the kitchen tap
and leans down over the sink and tilts his head sideways
to drink directly from the stream of cool water,
I think of my older brother, now almost ten years gone,
who used to do the same thing at that age;

and when he lifts his head back up and, satisfied,
wipes the water dripping from his cheek
with his shirtsleeve, it's the same casual gesture
my brother used to make; and I don't tell him
to use a glass, the way our father told my brother,

because I like remembering my brother
when he was young, decades before anything
went wrong, and I like the way my son
becomes a little more my brother for a moment
through this small habit born of a simple need,

which, natural and unprompted, ties them together
across the bounds of death, and across time ...
as if the clear stream flowed between two worlds
and entered this one through the kitchen faucet,
my son and brother drinking the same water.

WALKING WITH ELIZA

Late morning, mid-October, Eliza and I
walk through the woods, the dog trotting
ahead one minute, then dawdling behind us
to sniff some pungent clump of damp leaves
before catching up with the two of us again.
We've both had birthdays this month—
fifty for me, a milestone I'm not sure
what to make of, for her fourteen,
a humbler number marking a transformation
more tangible: her tomboy phase finally over,
the baseball cap she wore backwards every day
now hanging on a hook in her bedroom,
already a relic, her thick hair grown out,
her body taller, balancing between
childhood and the exciting, slightly frightening
unknown of what comes next. But for now,
she's collecting leaves: the yellow mittens
of the sassafras, the burgundy oaks,
the lemony ovals of the beeches baking
to brown, and the maples' red flamelets
scattered on the path, their backs a pale violet.
She says she likes the maples best, reminding me
of the time, some fifteen years ago,
when I said something like that to a friend
from out West, who scolded me for having
"a proprietary attitude toward nature."
I don't recount that story for Eliza
but instead say something about how funny it is
that we talk in a way that makes value judgments
about nature even though we know one thing
isn't "better" than another. She agrees, and adds,
"I like the other leaves, too,"—maybe that's
what I should have said to my friend! So simple.

I comment on how strange the weather is,
as if the day can't decide whether it wants
to rain or be sunny—and then on how funny
it is that we say things like that, as if the day
had feelings. I ask her if they've talked about this
in English class, and she says, "You mean
personification?" and I say yeah, deciding
to spare her the term "pathetic fallacy,"
another rule about how we're supposed to think,
a censoring of the imagination.
I'm balancing between my fatherly instinct
to teach her and my delight in the fresh way
she sees things, grateful to have her with me
to keep me from being weighed down
by my own thoughts like these rocks half-buried
in the trail. They're beaded with moisture,
and I say this must have something to do
with the way the day is both humid and cool.
Eliza says, "I like to think they're sweating,"
and I laugh and say, "Personification again,"
and talk about the difference between rational
and magical thinking, and how it's funny
that I, a poet, gave the scientific explanation
though I prefer to see it the other way,
or maybe both ways at once. Because, after all,
we're both Libras, always weighing
both sides of everything—for instance,
the ways she is like me and the ways she isn't,
and how I want her to stay as light
as the bag of leaves she's carrying
but know she won't be able to forever . . .
and the two of us continue walking together,
years apart but right next to each other,
dropping bits of conversation onto one
side of the scale or the other, talking
about this and that, pausing to call the dog.

CROSS-FERTILIZATION

It's come to this: I'm helping flowers have sex,
crouching down on one knee to insert
a Q-tip into one freckled foxglove bell
after another, without any clue
as to what I'm doing—which, come to think of it,
is always true the first time with sex.
And soon Randy Newman's early song
"Maybe I'm Doing It Wrong" is running
through my head as I fumble and probe,
golden pollen tumbling off the swab.

I transported these foxgloves from upstate New York,
where they grow wild, to our backyard
in Massachusetts, and I want them to multiply,
but the bumblebees, their main pollinators,
haven't found them, and I'm not waiting around.
The only diagram I found online portrayed
a flower in cross section, the stamens extending
the loaded anthers toward the flared opening,
but the text explained, "The female sexual
organs are hidden." Of course they are.

Which leaves me in the dark, transported back
to a state of awkward if ardent
unenlightenment, a complete beginner
figuring it out as I go along,
giggling a little and humming an old song
as I stick the Q-tip into another flower
as if to light the pilot of a gas stove
with a kitchen match, leaning in to listen for
the small quick gasp that comes
when the flame makes contact with the source.

ACKNOWLEDGMENTS

Many thanks to the editors and staff of the following publications in which these poems first appeared, sometimes in slightly different form.

The Academy of American Poets (Poem-A-Day series, www.poets.org): "Enough" and "The Figure on the Hill"
AGNI online: "On Bitching"
The American Poetry Review: "Walking with Eliza"
The American Scholar: "Island, 1979"
The Chattahoochee Review: "After Reading Han Shan," "Kingfisher," and "Separation Anxiety"
Chautauqua Literary Journal: "Remembering Karenia Brevis"
Cimarron Review: "Pump"
Columbia Magazine: "Light Snow" and "Out Back"
The Common: "Cross-Fertilization," "A Drink of Water," "Nobody Died," and "Two Salukis"
Connotation Press: "Out Walking"
Green Mountains Review: "Afterword" and "You Don't Put Flowers in Poems"
The Hat: "Alice Neel's Soirée"
The Hudson Review: "Banister," "Before the Play," "The Day You Looked upon Me as a Stranger," "The Day Nothing Happened," and "Listening to Virginia"
The New Criterion: "Smokehouse"
New England Review: "Essay on a Recurring Theme"
New Ohio Review: "Commuter Buddhist" and "Slip"
The New Republic: "For Clare" and "Renewal"
Ploughshares: "Danger: Tulips"
Plume: "Poem"
Poetry London: "The Same River" and "Vision"
Poetry Northwest: "Creature Comforts," "Custody of the Eyes," and "Natural History of the Yard"
Shenandoah: "The Digestive Fallacy"
The Southern Review: "Magatama" and "Roofer"
Southwest Review: "Mailboxes in Late Winter" and "The Shoulders of Women"
The Spoon River Poetry Review: "Work"
TriQuarterly: "Ivan Ilyich at the Lake," "Learning the Trails," and "Shaking Off the Snow"
upstreet: "Brief Note for April's Departure," "Nest," "Temple," "Temporary Blindness," and "To a Snake"
The Yale Review: "Encounter with John Malkovich" and "The Generations"

Thanks also to the editors of the *Alhambra Poetry Calendar*, *Cave Wall*, and *The Warwick Review* (U.K.), where several of these poems also appeared.

"Nest" and "Mailboxes in Late Winter" were also featured on the Poetry Foundation's website *American Life in Poetry* (www.americanlifeinpoetry.org). Thanks to Ted Kooser and Patricia Emile.

"Nest" also appears in *The Waiting Room Reader II: Words to Keep You Company* (edited by Rachel Hadas, CavanKerry Press, 2013).

"Essay on a Recurring Theme" also appears in *Obsession: Sestinas for the 21st Century* (edited by Carolyn Beard Whitlow and Marilyn Krysl, University Press of New England, 2014).

"Listening to Virginia" is reprinted in *The Pushcart Prize XXXVIII: Best of the Small Presses*, 2014 Edition.

For comments that helped to shape these poems and this book, I am grateful to Karen Chase, Robert Cording, Alan Feldman, David Ferry, Jessica Greenbaum, David Henry, Carol Moldaw, Stanley Plumly, Lewis Robinson, Peter Schmitt, and Tom Sleigh. Thanks also, for their helpful suggestions, to Chard deNiord, Keith Dunlap, Tom Gettler, Edward Hirsch, Eric Karpeles, Francesco Rognoni, Jane Shore, and Charlie Worthen. Love and gratitude to Julie, William, and Eliza.

See our complete backlist at www.tupelopress.org